MONARCHY

Sovereignty of a King or Queen

SYSTEMS OF GOVERNMENT

Systems of Government

MONARCHY
Sovereignty of a King or Queen

Larry Gillespie

MASON CREST
PHILADELPHIA

Mason Crest
450 Parkway Drive, Suite D
Broomall, PA 19008
www.masoncrest.com

© 2019 by Mason Crest, an imprint of National Highlights, Inc.

All rights reserved. No part of this publication may be reproduced or transmitted in any form or by any means, electronic or mechanical, including photocopying, recording, taping, or any information storage and retrieval system, without permission from the publisher.

Printed and bound in the United States of America.

CPSIA Compliance Information: Batch #GOV2018.
For further information, contact Mason Crest at 1-866-MCP-Book.

First printing
1 3 5 7 9 8 6 4 2

Library of Congress Cataloging-in-Publication Data

    Names: Gillespie, Larry, 1965- author.
    Title: Monarchy : sovereignty of a king or queen / Larry Gillespie.
    Description: Philadelphia : Mason Crest Publishers, 2019. | Series: Systems
      of government | Includes bibliographical references and index. | Audience:
      Grade 7 to 8.
    Identifiers: LCCN 2017056993 (print) | LCCN 2017052203 (ebook) | ISBN
      9781422277720 (ebook) | ISBN 9781422240205 (hc)
    Subjects: LCSH: Monarchy—Juvenile literature.
    Classification: LCC JC375 (print) | LCC JC375 .G55 2019 (ebook) | DDC
      321/.609—dc23
    LC record available at https://lccn.loc.gov/2017056993

Systems of Government series ISBN: 978-1-4222-4014-4

QR CODES AND LINKS TO THIRD-PARTY CONTENT

You may gain access to certain third party content ("Third-Party Sites") by scanning and using the QR Codes that appear in this publication (the "QR Codes"). We do not operate or control in any respect any information, products, or services on such Third-Party Sites linked to by us via the QR Codes included in this publication, and we assume no responsibility for any materials you may access using the QR Codes. Your use of the QR Codes may be subject to terms, limitations, or restrictions set forth in the applicable terms of use or otherwise established by the owners of the Third-Party Sites. Our linking to such Third-Party Sites via the QR Codes does not imply an endorsement or sponsorship of such Third-Party Sites, or the information, products, or services offered on or through the Third- Party Sites, nor does it imply an endorsement or sponsorship of this publication by the owners of such Third-Party Sites.

Table of Contents

KEY ICONS TO LOOK FOR:

Words to understand: These words with their easy-to-understand definitions will increase the reader's understanding of the text while building vocabulary skills.

Sidebars: This boxed material within the main text allows readers to build knowledge, gain insights, explore possibilities, and broaden their perspectives by weaving together additional information to provide realistic and holistic perspectives.

Educational Videos: Readers can view videos by scanning our QR codes, providing them with additional educational content to supplement the text. Examples include news coverage, moments in history, speeches, iconic sports moments and much more!

Text-dependent questions: These questions send the reader back to the text for more careful attention to the evidence presented there.

Research projects: Readers are pointed toward areas of further inquiry connected to each chapter. Suggestions are provided for projects that encourage deeper research and analysis.

Series glossary of key terms: This back-of-the-book glossary contains terminology used throughout this series. Words found here increase the reader's ability to read and comprehend higher-level books and articles in this field.

Prince William and his new bride, Kate Middleton, greet a crowd of well-wishers after their wedding, April 29, 2011.

 Words to Understand in This Chapter

absolute monarchy—a form of government in which the monarch holds power that is not limited by laws or a constitution.

constitution—a document that contains the system of fundamental laws and principles that determines the nature, functions, and limits of a government.

constitutional monarchy—a system of government in which a monarch is guided by a constitution that specifies his or her rights, duties, and responsibilities.

coronation—the act or ceremony of crowning a monarch.

dynasty—a line of hereditary rulers; a succession of monarchs who are related to or members of the same family.

parliament—a legislative assembly or lawmaking body.

parliamentary democracy—a political system with an elected parliament, in which a prime minister serves as head of government.

primogeniture—the law determining succession: the throne is passed down to the firstborn child.

regalia—the emblems or symbols of royalty.

Traditions of the Monarchy

In the spring of 2011 an estimated 2 billion people around the world were riveted by a televised wedding. The event, attended by 1,900 guests, took place with pomp and pageantry and images of scarlet-and-gold uniformed soldiers on horseback before an old Gothic church. It was a royal wedding, held at the 700-year-old Westminster Abbey, in London, England.

When the ceremony was over, 28-year-old Prince William, Duke of Cambridge, had wed Catherine "Kate" Middleton. With their marriage, Kate, who has no royal blood, became a duchess and a member of the royal family. The wedding thrilled the estimated one million people who thronged the streets outside the abbey, as well as millions more who celebrated at parties in England that night. The royal wedding allowed

Key Idea

A monarchy is a form of government in which a sovereign ruler, usually determined by hereditary succession and usually serving for life, is head of state. The powers of most monarchies today are limited by constitutions or parliaments.

them to show support for the British monarchy, an English institution that dates back more than a thousand years.

William is a member of the Windsor *dynasty*. His grandparents are Queen Elizabeth II—who currently sits on the British throne—and Philip, the Duke of Edinburgh. His father, Charles, the Prince of Wales, is first in line for the throne upon the death of the queen. William is second in line to the British throne.

What Is a Monarchy?

The titles of king and queen, prince and princess, duke and duchess, earl and countess are used in a form of government known as a monarchy. The word *monarchy* comes from the Greek language: *monarkhia* means "rule of one." In a monarchy, a *sovereign* serves as head of state, holding power until his or her death or abdication.

The title of a male monarch may be king, emperor, shah, caliph, sultan, emir, or tsar, while the title of a female leader is usually queen or empress. Monarchs differ from other heads of state, such as presidents, because their position is typically unelected and held for life.

Rules of succession determine who is to be the next king or queen. In many cases, succession is determined by *primogeniture*. This is a system of hereditary monarchy in which the eld-

Queen Elizabeth II and her husband, Prince Philip, the Duke of Edinburgh, wave from the balcony at Buckingham Palace in London. In 2017 the queen celebrated 65 years on the British throne. She ascended to the throne on February 6, 1952, upon the death of her father. She is the longest-serving British monarch in history.

Educational Video

For a short video explaining the origins of absolute monarchy, scan here:

ABSOLUTE MONARCHIE

est child is first in line to the throne. In the past, patrilineal primogeniture was the rule in most countries with monarchies. This meant only sons could ascend to the throne.

The right to rule is sometimes based on proximity of blood, or closeness in degree of kinship. In such cases a younger brother or nephew succeeds the king. When a succession of rulers of a kingdom or nation are related to or are members of the same family, they are considered part of a dynasty.

Rules of succession were designed to ensure continuity of leadership and government stability. When a monarch died, everyone knew who would lead next. This prevented potentially violent struggles for power. In England, acceptance of the rules of succession was expressed by the statement "The King is dead. Long live the King!"

Monarchy evolved in human history as states became larger and more complex. It allowed for strong, centralized government. History offers many examples of kings and queens who ruled effectively, bringing benefits to their societies. But there

are also many examples of weak, frivolous, or corrupt monarchs whose reigns proved disastrous. Such cases show the weakness of a system in which governing authority is treated as a birthright.

Forms of Monarchies

Monarchies are not all the same. The power of a sovereign can vary from nation to nation.

An *absolute monarchy* is a monarchy that is not limited by the laws or *constitution* of the nation. The head of state holds absolute authority. He or she has the power to make, enforce, and interpret the laws, as well as determine punishments. In an absolute monarchy the king or queen rules by decree and

Sultan Qaboos bin Said of Oman is an absolute monarch. He controls all powers of government, and his authority is not limited by a constitution or set of laws.

answers to no judicial, legislative, religious, or electoral body.

A *constitutional monarchy* is a system of government in which the monarch has limited powers, which are specified by the nation's constitution or laws. In such systems, the authority to create new laws rests with a *parliament*, assembly, or some other legislative body. Usually the head of government is a prime minister, chief minister, or premier. In some constitu-

King Willem-Alexander (right) and Queen Maxima of the Kingdom of the Netherlands attend a ceremony. Willem-Alexander succeeded his mother, Queen Beatrix, when she abdicated her role as monarch in 2013.

tional monarchies today, the monarch has significant powers (for example, the authority to dissolve the legislature or veto laws). But in most cases the king or queen is a figurehead who performs only ceremonial functions.

In addition to being a constitutional monarchy, the United Kingdom is also a *parliamentary democracy*. The British Parliament is a legislative body with two chambers: the House of Commons and the House of Lords. Most laws originate in the House of Commons, whose 650 members are elected by the people. The head of the political party with the majority of

seats in the House of Commons is the prime minister. Parliament's other chamber, the House of Lords, revises and approves legislation. It has approximately 825 members (the exact number can vary at any given time). In the past, the House of Lords was the exclusive domain of the aristocracy: only those with an inherited title of nobility had seats. Today, most members of the House of Lords are appointed and have "life peerages"—titles, conferred by the monarch for exceptional achievement, that cannot be passed on to children.

The Aristocracy

Throughout history, monarchs governed countries with the help of family members and a small class of wealthy elites, known as the aristocracy. The aristocracy, which was usually made up of the hereditary nobility, might manage estates, control the military, or collect taxes. Other nobles served as advisers to the monarch or helped deal with affairs of the country, including its finances, foreign relations, defense, and laws.

This ruling class, along with the king's advisers and courtiers, made up the royal court. A monarch typically "held court" at the sovereign's official residence, the palace. But politics was not the only focus. Royal courts were also places where new ideas in literature, science, and fashion would be discussed and displayed. Royal families and the aristocracy also established rites and rituals that formed the traditions of a monarchy.

Symbols, Rites, and Rituals

One of the most important traditions for the British royal fam-

ily is the *coronation* ceremony, a ritual that officially authorizes a monarch's right to rule. Coronations often have a religious component. In Britain, for example, the Archbishop of Canterbury—the senior bishop and principal leader of the Church of England—presides over the ceremony.

The ritual typically includes the use of certain "crown jewels"—the crowns, ornaments, and other jewelry acquired during the existence of the institution. These items can be of great value, skillfully crafted of gold or silver and studded with precious gems. Crown jewels are also worn or carried for state occasions. Such *regalia* serve the purpose of connecting the present ruler with the history and traditions of the past. Their use represents the continuity of the monarchy.

In Britain, the coronation ritual has remained basically the same for a thousand years. It begins with the new sovereign being presented to and acclaimed by the people. After being shown certain crown jewels symbolizing the authority of the monarchy, the new king or queen is asked to swear an oath promising to uphold the law, justice, and the Church. After affirming the oath, the monarch is anointed with oil, presented with more regalia, and crowned. Afterward, the new king or queen receives oaths of loyalty, or homage, from subjects of the *realm.*

At the coronation of Queen Elizabeth II, held in June 1953, the archbishop placed St. Edward's crown (created in 1661) on her head. At the end of the ceremony, she removed the coronation crown and replaced it with the Imperial State Crown. Wearing that crown, she walked out of Westminster Abbey carrying in her left hand a hollow golden sphere, called the

The royal coat of arms of the United Kingdom includes symbols that represent the lands ruled by the monarch: the lion (England), unicorn (Scotland), and a harp (Northern Ireland).

The temples, monuments, and palaces built or used by a ruler are another indication of a monarch's power and authority. In Britain, the official residences of the queen include Buckingham Palace, in London (pictured); Windsor Castle, in Berkshire, England; and the Palace of Holyroodhouse, in Edinburgh, Scotland.

Sovereign's Orb, and a jewel-ornamented golden rod, called the Scepter with the Cross, in her right.

The queen also wears the Imperial State Crown on occasions such as the State Opening of Parliament. This annual ritual, which follows a centuries-old tradition, requires the monarch to deliver before Parliament a speech on the country's plans and future laws. The speech is written by the prime minister.

Another symbol of the monarchy is the royal coat of arms—the shield representing the British monarchy. Because the duty of a ruler is to guarantee that justice is done, the royal coat of arms appears in courtrooms throughout the United Kingdom.

Details of the coat of arms also appear on coins that feature the portrait of the queen. An important symbol of the monar-

chy is the image of its sovereign. Early civilizations used statues and monuments to represent the power of the monarchy. Later kingdoms issued coins and paper money stamped with a sovereign's portrait as proof of his or her authority. Today, the image of Queen Elizabeth appears on coins, paper currency, and stamps.

In constitutional monarchies the sovereign and his or her family often play a ceremonial role in many of the country's military, political, and diplomatic functions. For many people they are a symbol of their nation's cultural identity.

 Text-Dependent Questions

1. What is the origin of the word *monarchy*?
2. What is primogeniture?
3. What are some differences between an absolute monarchy and a constitutional monarchy?

 Research Project

Using your school library or the internet, research some other forms of government, such as democracy, oligarchy, or dictatorship. What are some ways that these forms of government are different from monarchy? Are there ways that they are similar? Make a list and share it with your class.

This detail from an ancient palace in Persepolis shows people bringing valuable gifts as tribute to the ruler of the Achaemenid empire of ancient Persia.

 Words to Understand in This Chapter

cuneiform—an ancient writing system used in Mesopotamia, which involved marking wedge-shaped characters on clay tablets.

epic poem—a long, narrative poem that is usually about heroic deeds and events that are significant to the culture of the poet.

natural phenomena—a general term for events that occur in nature, such as sunrises and sunsets, powerful storms, rainbows, tides, earthquakes, and volcanic activity.

republic—a democratic form of government in which elected representatives vote on legislation and in which the head of state isn't a monarch but is usually a president.

2 Ancient Monarchies

Monarchy is one of the oldest forms of government. It began in early civilizations in North Africa and Asia where agricultural communities were headed by tribal chiefs. These villages evolved into cities and city-states with large populations. With the rise of these urban centers came monarchies.

The authority of monarchs helped bring order to society. Kings (and, on very rare occasions, queens) commanded armies that protected the resources of the kingdom, particularly land and access to fresh water. Monarchs led battles to build and maintain their kingdom's supremacy. They arranged for public works such as the building of roads, bridges, and temples. And they served as spiritual leaders.

The monarch's subjects included priests, soldiers, administrators, craftsmen, and farmers. The lower classes—the crafts-

men and farmers—typically supported ruling classes by paying taxes and tribute to the king.

Mesopotamian Kings

Mesopotamia—the land between the Tigris and Euphrates Rivers in today's Iraq—is often referred to as the cradle of civilization. The first city-states that developed in the region were part of the Sumerian civilization. By 3000 BCE many of these city-states contained populations of 30,000 to 40,000 people.

Each Sumerian city-state had its own royal dynasty, gods, and temples. Mesopotamian kings, who served as high priests, were believed to rule with divine assistance. They governed for the gods, but generally were not considered to be gods.

An exception to that idea was a Sumerian king named Gilgamesh. The fifth king of Uruk, a city-state located on the Euphrates River, ruled around 2700 BCE. His story is told in an *epic poem* called the *Epic of Gilgamesh*. In the poem, Gilgamesh is described as part god, and part human. He is also credited with building the great walls that surrounded and protected the city of Uruk. The *Epic of Gilgamesh* is one of the earliest recorded works of literature. It is written in cuneiform, the oldest known written language.

Over the years, the Sumerian

 Ancient Writing

Writing developed independently in the cities of Mesopotamia, Egypt, China, and Central America. It was first used for recordkeeping, which was essential for monarchs governing large cities. Early writings typically recorded the day-to-day administration of tasks of state, which included running large temples and tracking the movement and storage of goods.

A portion of the Code of Hammurabi, an ancient collection of laws created by a Mesopotamian king more than 3,700 years ago.

city-states fought among themselves for dominance. Around 2300 BCE they were conquered by kings of the Akkadian Empire. The founding king of these unified city-states in Mesopotamia was Sargon, who reigned from around 2334 to 2279 BCE. He and his descendants introduced the concept of "divine kingship," the idea that the king was a god or a representative of the gods. The empire collapsed around 2100 BCE.

Another major power in Mesopotamia was the Babylonian Empire. It originated with the city-state of Babylon, founded in

the late third or early second millennium BCE on the banks of the Euphrates River. Under King Hammurabi, who ruled from around 1792 to 1750 BCE, the city-state expanded into an empire. As king, Hammurabi worked to develop rules of law. He produced the first known written set of laws, known as the Code of Hammurabi. Almost three hundred laws and legal decisions were inscribed on several tall stone pillars, called stelae, for public display in Babylonian cities. They were written in both *cuneiform* script and in the Akkadian language.

Egyptian Pharaohs

Around 3000 BCE a powerful civilization was also developing in Egypt, where cities had sprung up along the Nile River. This fertile land in North Africa was ruled by pharaohs of 31 different dynasties during the period 3100–30 BCE.

According to historical records Menes (also known as Narmer) was the first pharaoh. He is credited with founding the Egyptian Empire by uniting the tribes of Upper and Lower Egypt into one kingdom.

Egypt saw some of its greatest prosperity during the third through sixth dynasties, which ruled from 2686 to 2125 BCE. During that time huge pyramids were built as tombs for the mummified bodies of the pharaohs and queens. The largest pyramid was constructed in Giza for King Khufu around 2540 BCE. It cov-

Key Quote

"What is the king of Upper and Lower Egypt? He is a god by whose dealings one loves, the father and mother of all men, alone by himself, without an equal."

—Egyptian hymn

The pyramids of Egypt were built as tombs and monuments for some of the most powerful pharaohs. More than 100 pyramids were built in Egypt between 4,000 and 4,500 years ago. Pyramids have been built in other places around the world as well.

Key Idea

In many ancient cultures the monarch was believed to connect ordinary people with their gods. Pharaohs and other monarchs identified themselves as gods, deserving of sacrifices and worship in their own right.

ered 13 acres and rose to a height of almost 500 feet. Known today as the Great Pyramid, it stood as a symbol of the power of the Egyptian king.

The pyramids reflected the pharaohs' status in Egyptian society as gods. Egyptian kings were considered divine beings with special powers over natural phenomena. People prayed and made sacrifices to the ruler. Belief in the pharaoh's divinity assured his or her absolute power.

Pharaohs, however, were not supposed to rule by whim. They were to abide by a concept called Ma'at. This was a spiritual principle of truth and justice, and especially of cosmic order and harmony. The pharaoh was regarded as the guardian of Ma'at, responsible for maintaining fundamental order and harmony. In this role, the ruler led important religious ceremonies and built temples to the Egyptian gods.

The Egyptian Empire was at its height from around 1550 to 1070 BCE, during the 18th, 19th, and 20th dynasties. At that time the Egyptian state included the Nile Valley from the Nile Delta to today's Sudan, stretching to the east to the borders of the Sinai Peninsula. The empire's efficient bureaucracy and great wealth enabled the continued building of pyramids and monuments, efficient running of its taxation systems, and mobilization of vast armies.

Most pharaohs were men. However, a few women did rule.

One was the 18th-dynasty pharaoh Hatshepsut, who reigned for 20 years (1479–1458 BCE). She oversaw many public works projects, including a great temple at Deir el Bahri near Thebes (Luxor), which was then the capital of Egypt. Famous male pharaohs of the 18th dynasty include Akhenaton and Tutankhamun.

A renowned pharaoh who ruled during Egypt's height was Ramesses II, of the 19th dynasty. During his long reign (ca. 1279–1213 BCE), Ramesses conquered lands to the north and south and erected colossal monuments that portrayed him as a strong leader and great pharaoh. Well after his death, he was still worshiped as a god.

Battles against foreign empires would weaken the Egyptian Empire. In 525 BCE Egypt was brought under the control of the

 Maurya Empire

One of India's greatest emperors was Ashoka Maurya, or Ashoka, who ruled from about 270 to 230 BCE. A successful military leader, he created and expanded an empire that included most of present-day India. But he is best known for renouncing war and embracing the Buddhist faith after one of his military campaigns resulted in the deaths of thousands of people.

To spread the word, Ashoka arranged for various teachings to be inscribed onto sculpted pillars and boulders. The Edicts of Ashoka, or Pillars of Ashoka, were placed throughout his realm. In this way, the king used his power to advance religious principles of nonviolence, respect, and tolerance and not his own glory. Although his empire broke up 50 years after his death, Ashoka remained an important inspiration because of his teachings.

Statue of Pharaoh Ramesses II at a temple in Abu Simbel, Egypt. Ranesses ruled Egypt around 3,200 years ago, and is considered one of the most powerful of the ancient pharaohs.

Achaemenid Empire. It fell to the Macedonian conqueror Alexander the Great in 332 BCE. Egypt's 31st and final dynasty would be founded in 305 BCE, when one of Alexander's generals, Ptolemy, declared himself pharaoh. The Ptolemaic dynasty gave Egypt its last pharaoh, Cleopatra VII. She killed herself in 30 BCE rather than be taken prisoner when Egypt was defeated by Rome.

Achaemenid Empire

Centered in today's Iran, the Achaemenid Empire (550–330 BCE) reached to Turkey and Egypt in the west and Afghanistan and Pakistan to the east. Sometimes known as the First Persian Empire, it was founded by Cyrus the Great.

Cyrus called himself Shahanshah, or "king of kings." He established an extensive network of roads and an efficient system of administering his far-flung empire. In distant provinces, a governor known as a satrap represented the king's authority. The satrap enforced law, levied taxes, and raised armies. The

The use of round-shaped metals as coins is said to have originated in Lydia, a kingdom founded around 1000 BCE, in today's western Turkey. King Croesus, who ruled in the sixth century BCE, is credited with issuing the first coins based on standards of weights and purity. As monarch, he guaranteed the value of the gold and silver currency produced by the Lydian kingdom. Such standards were not in place in the rest of the world, so Croesus's coins were used well beyond the borders of the kingdom.

system enabled the multicultural military power of the Achaemenid Empire to last more than 200 years.

Macedonian Empire

Ancient Macedonia, located in the northeastern area of modern-day Greece, became a military power under the rule of Philip II. After Philip's assassination in 336 BCE, the king was succeeded by his 20-year-old son, Alexander.

Within 12 years Alexander the Great, as he is known today, had amassed a vast empire. It included Greece, lands of the Persian Empire, Egypt, the Middle East (today's Turkey, Iraq, Syria, and Egypt), and territories that stretched to northwestern India. Alexander also assumed the title of Pharaoh of Egypt and King of the Persians (which he took from Darius III, the last king of the Achaemenid Empire).

Alexander claimed to be descended from the mythical Greek hero Heracles. And many of the people his armies conquered considered him a living god. But in 323 BCE he showed that he was indeed mortal, dying

The Macedonian ruler Alexander the Great was the greatest conqueror of the ancient world. At the time of his death in 323 BCE, his empire included large portions of southeastern Europe, Egypt, and central Asia.

Educational Video

Scan here to see what happened to Alexander's empire after his death:

from an illness or possible poisoning at the age of 32. After a series of civil wars, control of Alexander's empire was eventually divided among four of his generals.

One of Alexander's former generals, Lysimachus, went on to rule Thrace (part of the Macedonian Empire that is today's Bulgaria, northern Greece, and Turkey). To legitimize his rule, he issued coins that featured Alexander's image. The coins portrayed the great warrior both as a man and as the god Zeus-Amon (a combination of the leading god of the Greeks and the leading god of the Egyptians). The coins were among the first to carry the likeness of a ruler.

Roman Empire

According to traditional sources, Rome was founded in 753 BCE by twin brothers named Romulus and Remus, with Romulus becoming king after his brother's death in a fraternal dispute. Six kings are said to have followed Romulus. The Roman monarchy, according to tradition, had an unusual feature: king-

ship wasn't inherited. Rather, kings were elected by members of the senate, an assembly of elders. Kings did serve for life, however. The monarchy is said to have ended in 509 BCE, when King Tarquin tried to establish a hereditary dynasty and was overthrown. Scholars aren't certain how much of the traditional account of the Roman monarchy is historically accurate. No written records exist before the mid-fourth century BCE—150 years after the supposed reign of Tarquin—and the archaeological evidence from the monarchical period is scant.

In any event, Rome became a *republic*, headed by two elected consuls. This system of government lasted for about 500 years until a powerful general named Julius Caesar took control of the government as dictator. After his assassination in 44 BCE, civil war broke out.

In 31 BCE Julius Caesar's grandnephew and heir, Octavian, ended the war by defeating Marc Antony and Cleopatra at the Battle of Actium in Egypt. A few years later, in 27 BCE, the Roman senate bestowed on Octavian the honorific title of Augustus (*August* means "the revered one"). Although he did not carry a scepter or wear a crown, Caesar Augustus assumed the power of an emperor. The Roman senate still existed, but it had little actual authority.

During Augustus's 40-year rule, the Roman Empire enjoyed a period of prosperity and peace. A great deal of construction took place in Rome and around the empire.

Like rulers before him, Augustus also made sure his image was before the public eye. Statues of him as a young warrior were erected throughout the empire, and his likeness was stamped on coins. This symbolic presence conveyed the emper-

The government established by Caesar Augustus, the first Roman emperor, led to a period known as the Pax Romana ("Roman peace"). During this prosperous period from 27 BCE to about CE 180, the government of the Roman Empire was stable and the imperial territories were mostly safe from foreign invaders.

or's power and inspired loyalty to Rome. Monarchies that followed would likewise use images and symbols in establishing their authority.

The Roman Empire dominated Europe for several centuries. Its emperors assumed great power. Many of these imperial rulers came to be worshiped as gods.

Olmec and Mayan Civilizations

While empires based on monarchy thrived in Asia, Africa, and Europe, they also came into existence in other parts of the world. One was in Central America, where the ancient Olmec civilization emerged around the southern Gulf Coast of Mexico. Often referred to as the mother culture of Central America, the Olmec

This ceramic figure, which represents a Mayan king, was created around CE 1100. It was found on Jaina Island, a burial site for elite members of Mayan society in the western Yucatan Peninsula.

civilization was the first in the region to build large cities. The culture flourished from around 1400 BCE to 400 BCE.

Olmec cities were ruled by kings and queens. Like the ancient Egyptians, the Olmecs buried their mummified rulers in pyramids and temple monuments. The Olmecs were an agri-

cultural society. Maize, or corn, was particularly important. Statues of the early kings showed their sacred power by portraying them wearing the ceremonial dress of the maize god.

Another major civilization of Central America was the Mayan culture. The Mayan civilization, which reached its peak between CE 250 and 900, was based in today's southern Mexico, Honduras, Belize, and Guatemala. Tens of thousands of people lived in its huge cities, which like the Olmec urban centers featured pyramids, public monuments, temples, and palaces. Their gods were connected to the natural world. Among the most important were those associated with corn, rain, and the sun.

Mayan monarchs were believed to be descendants of the gods. In religious ceremonies kings and queens performed animal and human sacrifices and bloodletting rites, including self-sacrifice, to try to make contact with the gods or their ancestors. Monarchs made such sacrifices to guarantee good harvests, celebrate victories in war, and ensure order in the world.

The Shang and Zhou Dynasties

A ruler's connection with the gods was also important on the other side of the world, in China. One of the first dynasties of China was the Shang dynasty, whose members ruled for about 500 years, from 1500 to 1050 BCE. Their rise to power coincided with the emergence of China's first large cities. Around 1000 BCE the Zhou, warriors from the central steppes of Asia, overthrew the Shang dynasty.

The Zhou (ca. 1050–256 BCE) were the first Chinese dynasty to establish belief in the Mandate of Heaven. This idea

The throne of the Chinese emperor, on display in the Hall of Central Harmony in Beijing's Forbidden City.

is that the gods approve and support the authority of a just monarch. When that mandate is withdrawn, a ruler loses the right to rule and can be removed. The Shang were defeated, the Zhou claimed, because they no longer held the Mandate of Heaven. The Zhou dynasty spread its empire far beyond the area previously ruled by the Shang. And it thrived longer than any other Chinese dynasty.

Future emperors of China would claim to rule with the gods' blessing, saying they held the Mandate of Heaven. Their governments faced distrust, however, when there were disasters such as floods, famines, or earthquakes. People believed that the gods were offended and the mandate had been withdrawn.

 Text-Dependent Questions

1. What Mesopotamian king created an influential code of laws more than 3,700 years ago?
2. What did Pharaoh Ramesses II accomplish during his reign?
3. What general gained control over the Roman government and ruled as a dictator until his assassination?

 Research Project

Using the internet or your school library, do research on one of the major empires of the ancient world, such as the empires of Mesopotamia or Egypt, the Achaemenid empire of Persia, or the Roman empire. Write a two-page report detailing the powers held by their kings or queens.

In the feudal system of Europe during the Middle Ages, a monarch's power depended on the ability of his or her subordinates, called vassals or barons, to defend their land. Castles were a critical part of the defenses. However, because the castle was one of the most important military technologies of the day, the king had the power to approve and manage construction of all stone castles within his realm.

 Words to Understand in This Chapter

calligraphy—decorative handwriting or handwritten lettering.

cosmopolitan—familiar with and at ease in many different countries and cultures.

mosque—a Muslim place of worship.

opulent—extremely luxurious, showing off a person's wealth.

3 Medieval Monarchies

During the third century CE, there were two main powers in western Asia and Europe, the Sasanian Empire and the Roman Empire. By the fifth century the western half of the Roman Empire would collapse, and the Eastern Roman Empire would dominate as the Byzantine Empire. At that time, both the Sasanian and Byzantine empires would be matched by a third power in India. These three early empires followed different faiths, and all three were headed by monarchs.

Religious Empires

A major Persian empire, the Sasanian Empire was a highly centralized state that included today's Iran and Iraq and stretched from modern Syria to Pakistan. Its people followed the

Zoroastrian faith, a religion in which twin gods—one good and one evil—engage in a never-ending struggle. The Sasanian kings were considered agents of the good god. Their central role was to impose "divine order" on "demonic chaos." The Sasanian Empire lasted for more than 400 years, from CE 224 to 651.

In northern India, the Gupta Empire was founded in the early fourth century CE and reached its height in the fifth century. The newly revived faith of Hinduism flourished under Gupta rule, as the kings sponsored the building of temples and emphasized their royal connection to the major Hindu deities, such as Vishnu and Shiva. However, the king was not himself considered a god. During the Gupta dynasty, the modern forms of Hinduism in India were established, and the arts and sciences flourished in the empire.

To the west of the Gupta Empire, Emperor Constantine I ruled the Roman Empire between 306 and 337. After converting to Christianity, Constantine began building Christian churches and promoting the Christian faith, which soon became the predominant religion of the Roman Empire.

In the year 395, the Roman Empire split into eastern and western halves, with two separate governments. One government ruled the west from Rome, but in less than a century that part of the empire broke apart into numerous kingdoms ruled by Germanic nobles. The Eastern Roman Empire remained intact and was renamed the Byzantine Empire. Its rulers reigned from the capital city of Constantinople, formerly known as Byzantium. The Christian-based empire included today's Turkey, Greece, the Balkans, and the Middle East.

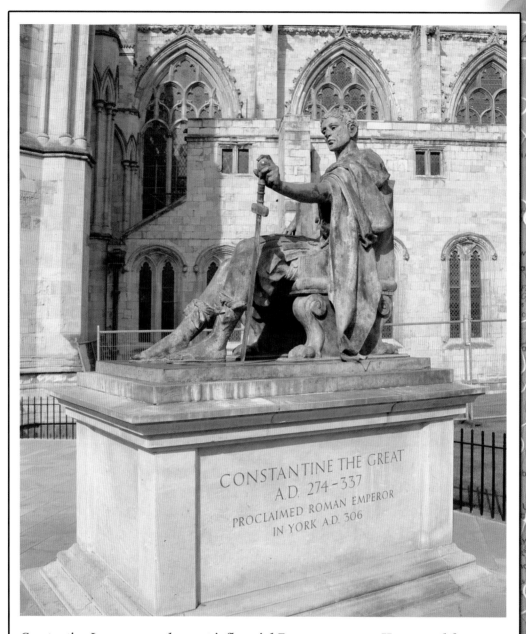

CONSTANTINE THE GREAT
A.D. 274-337
PROCLAIMED ROMAN EMPEROR
IN YORK A.D. 306

Constantine I was among the most influential Roman emperors. He emerged from a power struggle in the early fourth century to take complete control over the empire around CE *324. He moved the center of imperial government to a new capital in Asia Minor (modern-day Turkey), which he called Constantinople.*

The Dome of the Rock is a Muslim shrine in Jerusalem. It was built on the orders of the Umayyad caliph Abd al-Malik, who ruled from 685 to 705 CE.

Islamic Caliphates

During the seventh century another new faith, Islam, took hold. It was founded in 622 by the Prophet Muhammad. From the Arabian Peninsula, Islam spread quickly—through conquest as well as voluntary conversion—across the Middle East and North Africa following Muhammad's death in 632. However, there was disagreement among followers of Islam, or Muslims, over who should succeed Muhammad as leader of the

Muslim community. Eventually this led to the formation of two separate branches of Islam, known as Sunni and Shia.

Islamic leaders were called caliphs. A caliph headed the Muslim political state, or caliphate, and was also considered leader of the *umma*, or community of believers. The first four caliphs were all close companions of Muhammad and were chosen for their piety.

The fifth caliph, Muawiyah, established dynastic rule over the Islamic caliphate. Muawiyah's Umayyad Caliphate lasted from 661 to 750, when it was overthrown by the Abbasids.

From the 8th to 10th centuries, the Abbasid Caliphate stretched from central Asia to Spain. The Abbasid caliphs controlled much of the Middle East and North Africa. Major Muslim cities of the time included Cairo, in Egypt; and Baghdad and Samarra, in Iraq. At different times, both

 Mongolian Empire

In 1206 Genghis Khan brought together tribes of the central Asian steppes in modern-day Mongolia, and was proclaimed ruler of all Mongols. (*Khan* means "emperor" or "king" in the Mongolian language.) During the 13th and 14th centuries, the renowned warrior-king and his descendants conquered the surrounding lands, creating a vast empire. It reached from eastern Europe to the Sea of Japan, and included large parts of Siberia in the north, the Indian subcontinent to the south, and the Middle East to the west.

Kublai Khan, the grandson of Genghis Khan, conquered China and founded the Yuan dynasty. It controlled China, along with Mongolia, from 1271 to 1368.

Baghdad and Samarra served as capitals of the empire. Abbasid caliphs built *opulent* palaces and places of worship, or *mosques*, in both cities.

Tang Dynasty

Another major empire of the early medieval world was China's Tang dynasty. Between 500 and 800 the Islamic caliphate and the Tang dynasty dominated the commercial trade of luxury goods throughout Asia and Africa. Such trade was made possible by the Silk Road, a network of roads that at its peak spanned 4,000 miles and connected the East with the Mediterranean world. Among the most valuable items traded were gold, precious stones, spices, and silk.

This painting on silk from 641 CE depicts the Chinese Emperor Taizong (seated, right) meeting with Ludongzan, the ambassador of Tibet. The Tang dynasty, which lasted from 618 to 907, is considered a golden era of ancient Chinese civilization.

The Tang dynasty, founded in 618, governed a great civilization of *cosmopolitan* cities and featured a huge bureaucratic class. Members of the civil service ran various ministries and oversaw public works, the economy, the military, and ceremonial rituals. Two important rulers of the dynasty were military and political leader Emperor Taizong, who reigned from 626 to 649, and Wu Zetian, who ruled from 690 to 705. She was the only woman ever to rule as an emperor in China.

During its mostly peaceful 290-year rule, the Tang dynasty saw a great blossoming of culture and the arts, especially poetry, painting, and *calligraphy*. There were also a number of significant scientific advances. The empire controlled parts of today's Korea, Manchuria, and northern Vietnam.

Japanese Monarchy

According to Japanese legend, the first Japanese emperor, Jimmu, was the great-grandson of Ninigi. He in turn was the grandson of the Japanese sun goddess Amaterasu. Ninigi supposedly established the throne in 660 BCE when Amaterasu made him descend from Heaven to bring peace to the Japanese islands. At that time the goddess gave Ninigi a sacred mirror that would allow him and his successors to speak with her. She also gave him a string of jewels and a sword. The imperial regalia of the mirror, jewels, and sword continue to be used in modern Japanese enthronement ceremonies. The three sacred objects traditionally symbolize the legitimacy and authority of the Japanese emperor.

In 894, during the Fujiwara dynasty (794–1185), Japanese emperors cut off contact and most trade with the rest of the

The samurai were skilled warriors in medieval Japan. Typically, samurai served a shogun, or regional warlord, who in turn promised allegiance and paid taxes to the emperor.

world. Japan would remain isolated for several centuries.

Early Middle Ages

In Europe the period from around 500 to 1000 is known as the Early Middle Ages (or, less frequently, the Dark Ages). With the fall of the Western Roman Empire, the stability that the empire had provided was gone. It was a time of violence and unrest, with local rulers battling one another and invasions from tribes such as the Vikings, who were fierce warriors from Scandinavia.

Ultimately, smaller kingdoms were united into larger ones based on the feudal system. This was a form of governing in which the king owned all the land in his realm, but gave large portions of it to men in exchange for their loyalty and the promise to provide military service.

The men who took the grant of a fiefdom became the king's vassals and were given titles such as duke, earl, viscount, or baron. The king's vassals also had vassals of their own: they granted other men land in exchange for their allegiance and support. There could be many levels of lords who had vassals committed to them.

While the nobility held their estates on behalf of the monarch, they depended on the peasants, or serfs, to live on and work the land. Farmers had to pay taxes to the lord in the form of livestock

 Key Quote

"The just and peaceful king carefully thinks about each case, and not despising the sick and poor of his people, speaks just judgments, putting down the wicked and raising the good."

—Medieval Treatise

or grains. Some serfs worked directly for the lord's family, in the grand house, or manor. By the 1100s the feudal system was in place throughout Europe.

Charlemagne

Many of the lands of the former Western Roman Empire would be reunited under Charlemagne. Also known as Charles the Great, Charlemagne was the king of the Franks, a Germanic tribe that lived in western Europe. During his rule, from 768 to 814, he expanded his Frankish kingdom. By the year 800, he had created an empire that included much of western and central Europe. Under the rule of Charlemagne, there was stability and order.

Charlemagne had converted to Christianity, and he worked to bring the faith to the lands he conquered. On Christmas Day in the year 800, Pope Leo III crowned Charlemagne, proclaiming him emperor of the Romans.

The association of political power with the spiritual authority of the Catholic Church would be very important in the Middle Ages. Around Charlemagne's time, coronation ceremonies in kingdoms and empires that had converted to Christianity began to include the religious ritual of anointment with holy chrism. (Chrism is a mixture of oil and aromatic resins.) The anointment symbolized sanctification or blessing, and it affirmed the king's role as a spiritual as well as a worldly leader. Anointment also implied that the right to rule came from God.

Charlemagne's empire didn't survive intact for very long after his death in 814. The empire was officially divided into

During the years he ruled western Europe, Charlemagne promoted learning and estab-lished an effective system of government.

Educational Video

Scan here for a short video explaining the feudal system in England.

WHY WOULD WILLIAM THE CONQUEROR WANT TO DIVIDE UP HIS LANDS?

HE HAD TO REWARD PEOPLE FOR THEIR HELP IN TAKING OVER ENGLAND.

HE COULD PAY THEM IN 'LAND'

ENGLAND WAS A HUGE COUNTRY TO CONTROL IN THE MIDDLE AGES. BY SPLITTING IT UP AND LETTING HIS BARONS TAKE CONTROL, IT COULD BE CONTROLLED MUCH EASIER, AND WITH MUCH LESS EXPENSE!

three kingdoms, each ruled by one of Charlemagne's grandsons, in 843. By the end of the century, these kingdoms had disintegrated into multiple smaller states.

Anglo-Saxons

Germanic tribes invaded Britain during the early Middle Ages. These tribes included the Angles, Saxons, and Jutes, who formed kingdoms headed by monarchs. Between 500 and 850, seven Anglo-Saxon kingdoms controlled southern, central, and eastern Britain: East Anglia, Essex, Kent, Mercia, Sussex, Northumbria, and Wessex.

One of the most renowned Anglo-Saxon kings was Alfred of Wessex, known as Alfred the Great. During his rule (871–899), Alfred organized a system of laws. He also successfully defended Wessex from Viking invaders.

Other Anglo-Saxon kingdoms didn't fare as well in the face of attacks by the Norse warriors. By 900 Vikings held lands in

the north and east of Britain. Wessex claimed lands in the south and west.

In 927 King Athelstan of Wessex, the grandson of Alfred the Great, defeated the Vikings. He set about building a unified kingdom of England, assuming the title King of All Britain. It was the first time the region was united, although the union did not last.

A United England

England would ultimately be united by William the Conqueror, a warrior from a region of northern France known as Normandy. In October 1066 William and his men invaded England. At the Battle of Hastings, William's army defeated the soldiers of the Anglo-Saxon king, Harold. The following December, a coronation ceremony held in Westminster Abbey legitimized William as king of England.

During his reign as William I (1066–1087), the Norman king combined Anglo-Saxon and Norman laws, customs, and institutions. He granted parcels of land to his knights and had them swear loyalty to him, thus introducing the feudal system to England. This allowed him to establish a strong centralized monarchy. (Such oaths of loyalty remain part of the British coronation service.)

For monarchs to stay in power, they needed the advice and support of the most powerful of their subjects—the nobility and senior clergy. William consulted with his vassals at meetings he convened known as Great Councils. Later English kings would include members of the clergy, such as bishops and abbots. Around the 1230s these councils became known as

This detail from the Bayeux Tapestry, an embroidered cloth made during the 11th century, shows King Harold II of England feasting in London with nobles who had supported his claim to the throne in early 1066. In the feudal system, noblemen promised to be loyal to the king and provide financial and military support. In turn the king gave these nobles, called vassals, property and promised to protect their rights.

Parliament. The name came from the Old French word *parlement*, which means "speaking."

Other English kings would also introduce changes to strengthen the monarchy. Henry II ruled from 1154 to 1189. During his reign he expanded the power of the royal courts by increasing the number of criminal cases tried in the king's court and transferring property cases from local courts to royal courts. These actions increased the amount of money that the

monarch controlled. And raising money was often a concern of medieval kings.

Henry II's son was Richard I, who ruled from 1189 to 1199. A gifted military leader, he spent most of his time on the battlefield. Known as Richard the Lionheart, he fought in France for land claimed by England. And he led armed expeditions to present-day Israel as part of the Crusades. The Crusades were a series of conflicts that took place from 1095 to 1272 as the Christian countries of Europe and the Byzantine Empire fought to win back the Holy Land from the Islamic caliphates.

During the 1100s and 1200s, the Ayyubid Caliphate ruled much of the Middle East. Richard fought against its founder, a great warrior known as Saladin. While Richard was away from England, his brother John claimed the throne, becoming king in 1199.

The Magna Carta

King John was an unpopular ruler. And his popularity decreased as the expenses incurred by conflicts with France forced him to raise taxes. After losing lands to France, John returned from battle to England in need of money. But when he demanded that his feudal barons pay an extra tax without their consent, they rebelled. In 1215 civil war broke out, and the barons confronted King John on the battlefield and forced him to sign the Magna Carta.

 French-Speakers

Early Norman kings of England were vassals to the king of France. Many spoke only French, while their subjects spoke Old English, the language of the Anglo-Saxons.

Rebellious English barons watch King John sign the Magna Carta, 1215.

This legal document guaranteed certain basic rights and other liberties for all free men in the kingdom. It limited the monarch's ability to raise funds. And it was the first formal document stating that the monarch was under the same rule of law as his people. John would later say he signed the Magna Carta under duress, and he refused to abide by the document. But he died soon after, in 1216, and was succeeded by his son, Henry III.

John's grandson, Edward I, whose reign began in 1272, was determined to unite England, Wales, and Scotland under his rule by force. He waged wars against rebels in Wales during the late 13th century, and then against Scottish rebels led by William Wallace and Robert the Bruce. Meanwhile, the role of Parliament in the government increased. To raise taxes to pay his armies, Edward had to convene Parliament. Because of the Magna Carta, Parliament—and not the monarch—had the authority to make legislation levying taxes.

 Text-Dependent Questions

1. What dynasty ruled China from 618 to 907?
2. Who was Charlemagne, and what did he accomplish?
3. What Norman king conquered England in 1066?
4. What did the Magna Carta guarantee to free men in England?

 Research Project

Read the text of the Magna Carta at the British Library website:
   https://www.bl.uk/magna-carta/articles/magna-carta-english-translation
Choose one of the articles of the Magna Carta. Write a one-page report explaining why the issue in that article is addressed within the document.

The German king Otto III is crowned Holy Roman Emperor in Rome, 996. His grandfather, Otto the Great, and father, Otto II, had previously held this title.

 # Words to Understand in This Chapter

circumnavigage—to sail or travel around something, such as the Earth.

divine right of kings—this was a belief that kings and queens have a God-given right to rule, and that rebellion against them is a sin. This belief was common through the seventeenth century in Europe.

emirate—a form of government similar to a monarchy or sultanate, in which power is in the hands of an emir, or ruler of a Muslim state.

4 Early Modern Empires

During medieval times the power of the Roman Catholic Church grew in western Europe. Based in Rome, the pope, as the Church's official leader, claimed authority over all Christians in Europe. This meant the pope had greater power than a king. Many monarchs did not agree. They believed their *divine right* to be king justified their right to final authority.

The Holy Roman Empire

Church authority was affirmed when Pope Leo III crowned Charlemagne in 800. But Charlemagne's empire broke apart in the decades after his death.

In the 960s Otto the Great, ruler of the kingdom of Germany, gained control of the kingdoms of Burgundy (in

Educational Video

For a short video explaining the "divine right of kings," scan here:

France) and Italy. He established a church-state alliance that reunited a portion of Charlemagne's empire, which became the Holy Roman Empire. In 962 Pope John XII crowned Otto as its emperor.

The Holy Roman Empire would last for several centuries. However, it was not a hereditary monarchy. Princes of Germanic kingdoms, or electors, selected the ruler of the German kingdom. And that person would be crowned by the pope as emperor.

Concern that popes were interfering in the selection of German kings led one of the emperors, Charles IV, to call for the passage of the Golden Bull of 1356. This legal decree by the Imperial Diet (an assembly of the Imperial Estates of the Holy Roman Empire) established details of the election process and specified the electors. Charles sponsored passage of the legal decree as a way to assert monarchal authority in German politics over the authority of the pope.

The Protestant Reformation

Emperors and kings were not alone is their disagreement with the policies of the Roman Catholic Church. In 1517 an Augustinian monk named Martin Luther protested Church practices by nailing a list of his grievances on the door of a Catholic cathedral in Wittenberg, Germany. That act led to religious division among Christians. In a movement known as the Reformation, Protestants separated from the Roman Catholic Church. They rejected the pope's claim to supreme authority in religious and political matters and created a separate branch of Christianity.

Martin Luther's attempt to reform the Roman Catholic Church resulted in a division among Christians and the creation of Protestant churches throughout Europe. As the authority of the Church over Europe was weakened, monarchs gained greater power over their lands.

The Reformation movement caused religious and political turmoil throughout Europe. During his reign from 1519 to 1556 the Holy Roman Emperor Charles V fought in religious wars that swept the continent. He struggled to hold the empire together as European kingdoms accepted Protestantism. At the same time he was also dealing with Turkish forces of the Ottoman Empire, which were attacking the Christian lands of the former Byzantine Empire

in the east.

Ottoman Empire

As Christianity grew in western Europe, the Middle East saw the rise of another Islamic empire. Osman I was a Turkish leader from a kingdom in the northwestern Anatolia region of today's Turkey. In 1299 he declared his *emirate*'s independence, thus founding the Ottoman dynasty. (An emirate is a kingdom headed by a Muslim ruler.) The Islamic leader quickly amassed an empire by conquering lands formerly controlled by the Christian Byzantine Empire.

The Ottoman sultans constructed fortresses like this one to control the Bosporus strait, a key waterway near their capital at Istanbul (formerly Constantinople).

As the Ottoman Empire continued to spread in the 1300s, its leaders assumed the title of sultan. The disciplined fighting forces of the Ottoman Empire ensured its rise as a superpower. Ottoman Turks conquered Constantinople and brought an end to the Byzantine Empire. Renamed Istanbul, the city became the new capital of the Ottoman Empire.

Last Emperor

The last Byzantine emperor was Constantine XI. He died in 1453, while fighting to defend Constantinople from Muslim armies led by the Ottoman sultan Mehmed II.

One of the most powerful Ottoman sultans was Suleiman I, whose reign began in 1520. By the time of his death 46 years later, the empire controlled North Africa and the eastern Mediterranean. This forced western Europeans to find trade routes by sea.

Suleiman developed and established new laws and created

The Safavid Empire

A rival to the Ottoman Empire was the unified Persian state known as the Safavid Empire. Founded in 1502, it eventually included the lands of modern Iran and Iraq, as well as parts of Turkey and Georgia. One of the most famous Safavid rulers was Shah Abbas I the Great, who reigned from 1587 to 1629. He opened up Persia to trade with western European nations, centralized the government, improved the civil service, and modernized the army. Under the Safavid rulers, Shia Islam was established as the region's official religion.

During the 16th century, the New World conquests of Spanish soldiers like Hernán Cortés, Francisco Pizarro, and Hernando de Soto, and the adventures of explorers like Ferdinand Magellan and Juan Cabrillo, helped make Spain's King Charles I the wealthiest ruler in Europe. (As Holy Roman Emperor, he was known as Charles V.)

an efficient civil service. The sultan, who lived at the same time as the English king Henry VIII and the Holy Roman Emperor Charles V, was known to Europeans as Suleiman the Magnificent.

A Changing World

A modern world was emerging by the 1600s. In Europe, advancement in the fields of arts, literature, science, and philosophy were part of a period that became known as the Renaissance.

It was also a time of exploration, as the rulers of the king-

 Native American Empires

In 1500 the Inca Empire was the largest in the world. More than 12 million people were part of the empire, which included today's Colombia, Chile, and other parts of western South America. Its capital city was Cusco, in today's Peru. The Incas raised food using irrigation projects and canals; in a region with mountainous terrain, crops grew on terraced fields. The civilization was a highly organized society with an extensive road network, abundant food, and a powerful military force.

Around the same time in Central America, another indigenous civilization was also flourishing. At its height in the early 1500s it stretched from today's southern Mexico to Guatemala, from the Atlantic Ocean to the Pacific. The Aztec civilization consisted mostly of city-states ruled by individual kings. Many of these cities featured pyramids, temples, and paved roads. Kings paid tribute to the Aztec emperor, in the form of cloth, jewelry, corn, or gold.

Spanish conquerors destroyed both the Aztec and Inca Empires. The Aztecs were defeated in 1521, the Incas in 1533.

doms of Portugal and Spain funded major oceangoing expeditions. In Spain the monarchy funded the voyage of Christopher Columbus in 1492. The young Spanish king Charles I, who was also the Holy Roman emperor Charles V, sponsored ships led by Ferdinand Magellan in 1519 as they *circumnavigated* the globe for the first time. The 1500s and 1600s saw vast exploration by Portuguese and Spanish sailors.

Reports about unknown lands helped foster a new age of learning for the Western world. And that learning was advanced by the development of technologies such as the printing press. Access to the written word encouraged a rise of literacy. As people became more informed, some of them questioned the role of the Catholic Church and the monarchy in their lives.

England's Tudor Kings

In the 15th century, rival branches of England's royal family—the House of Lancaster and the House of York—fought a series of conflicts for the throne. In 1485 Henry Tudor of the House of Lancaster brought the 30-year-long Wars of the Roses to an end by defeating his rival, King Richard III of the House of York. Henry assumed the throne as King Henry VII, and founded

Henry Tudor's victory at the Battle of Bosworth Field in 1485 ended a civil war. He ruled England for nearly 24 years.

the Tudor dynasty. His court promoted the ideas and learning of the Renaissance. And as monarch Henry assumed greater control over the country's administration and coffers. His shrewd accounting practices ensured that the monarchy was adequately funded.

The religious division due to the Reformation peaked in England during the time of Henry VII's son, King Henry VIII, who reigned from 1509 to 1547. In his desire to divorce his queen, Catherine of Aragon, he broke away from the Roman Catholic Church. He dissolved Catholic monasteries in the country and seized their property. And he established the Church of England and declared himself its head, thus making him both a political and religious ruler.

During the reign of Queen Elizabeth I, the last of the Tudor monarchs, England asserted itself as an international economic and military power.

Henry VIII claimed that he ruled with the approval of God. He maintained the title of *Fidei Defensor*, or Defender of the Faith, first bestowed on him by the pope. But he no longer defended the Roman Catholic Church. Instead the title represented the role of the English monarch as defender of the Church of England.

Key Quote

"[Kings are] God's anointed, not in respect of the oil which the bishop useth, but in consideration of their power, which is ordained, of their sword, which is authorized, of their persons, which re elected by God, and indued with the gifts of his Spirit for the better ruling and guiding of his people."
—Archbishop Cranmer to Edward VI, 1547

After Henry's death in 1547 all three of his children would assume the throne. Edward VI died within a few years, and his sister Mary I succeeded him. A devout Catholic, she and her husband, Philip II of Spain, persecuted Protestants, causing religious turmoil throughout England. After Mary's death in 1558 Elizabeth, who was Protestant, ascended the throne.

Elizabeth's 45-year reign would become known as the Golden Age of England. During this time William Shakespeare wrote his famous plays and Sir Francis Drake explored the New World. After the British navy defeated the powerful Spanish Armada in 1588, the world viewed the nation with respect. In a speech before the troops defending the land, Elizabeth I affirmed her dedication to her country, saying, "I know I have but the body of a weak and feeble woman; but I have the heart of a king, and of a king of England too."

England's Constitutional Monarchy

After Elizabeth's death in 1603, King James VI of Scotland succeeded to the throne, ruling over both England and Scotland. His son Charles I, who became king in 1625, would bring the country to civil war.

Charles believed that his was an absolute monarchy.

Native American Empires

In a speech to England's Parliament in 1609, King James I explained his belief in the power of the monarchy.

> Kings are justly called Gods, for that they exercise a manner or resemblance of divine power upon Earth," the king said. "God hath power to create or destroy, make or unmake at His pleasure, to give life, or send death, to judge all, and to be judged nor accountable to none. . . . and the like power have kings: they make and unmake their subjects, they have power of raising, and casting down, of life and of death, judges over all their subjects, an din all causes, and yet accountable to none but God only.

Instead of working with Parliament, as previous kings had done, he fought against it. In 1629 he dissolved the legislative body. He did not call Parliament into session again until 1640. Their conflicts over taxation and control of the military led in 1642 to the English Civil War, between Royalists and Parliamentarians. After losing the war, Charles I was tried, found guilty of treason, and beheaded in 1649. He was the first British monarch to be executed for treason.

The British monarchy was abolished, and a Council of State headed by Oliver Cromwell was set up. But the new government did not last. Eleven years later, in 1660, Parliament restored the monarchy.

In 1689 Parliament asserted authority over King William III and Queen Mary II when it passed the Bill of Rights. The set of laws regulated the relationship between the monarch and the people. It limited powers of the king and guaranteed rights

of Parliament, including freedom of speech, the requirement to hold regular elections, and the right to petition the monarch without fear of retribution. The Bill of Rights also required that the Crown seek the consent of the people, as represented in Parliament. The document essentially made Britain a constitutional monarchy.

England and Scotland merged into one kingdom in 1707, and the country became known as Great Britain. Its first prime minister, Robert Walpole, came to power in 1721.

Divine Kings

The beheaded king, Charles I, was one of many medieval monarchs in England and France who believed that divine authority from God gave them the ability to heal the sick with their touch. They believed they could cure people stricken with the disease known as scrofula, or the King's Evil, by placing their hands around the swellings caused by the infection. Kings and queens arranged meetings with hundreds of afflicted people at a time in order to "heal" them with a royal touch. Some of these rulers included the English monarchs Charles I and Queen Anne, who came to the throne in 1702. French kings continued the practice until as late as 1825.

Absolute Monarchies

Although absolute monarchy did not take hold in Great Britain, it succeeded in other European countries during the 17th and 18th centuries. This was particularly true in France, Spain, Prussia, and Austria. The monarchs of these states ruled autocratically, holding supreme rule in both lawmaking and

policymaking. Rulers continued to justify this power as their divine right. They and many of their subjects believed that God had chosen them to serve the land.

King Louis XIV of France, who reigned from 1643 to 1715, best exemplified an absolute ruler. During his reign he weakened the power of the nobles, while increasing his own authority. He justified his rule by saying, "L'état, c'est mois," or "I am the state." The king paid little attention to the needs of his nation's people. Instead he lived extravagantly, spending exorbitant amounts of money on his royal court in Versailles, outside Paris.

 Text-Dependent Questions

1. What was the Holy Roman Empire?
2. What dynasty was founded in England by Henry VII after the Battle of Bosworth Field?
3. How did Britain's parliament assert authority over the monarch in 1689?

 Research Project

Using your school library or the internet, find out more about the Protestant Reformation. How did the effort to reform abuses by the Roman Catholic Church change the political landscape of Europe? How did monarchs react to the Reformation in Europe during the sixteenth and seventeenth centuries? Detail your research in a two-page paper.

French revolutionaries storm the Bastille, July 1789. To many common people of the time, this fortress-prison in Paris represented the abuses of the monarch, King Louis XVI.

 Words to Understand in This Chapter

abdicate—to renounce one's claim to the throne.

referendum—a vote by the people on a specific question.

regent—a person who rules when a monarch is a child or is incapacitated.

sultanate—a government in which the supreme power is in the hands of a sultan (the head of a Muslim state).

5 The Decline of the Monarchy

During the late 1600s and 1700s Europe saw the rise of an intellectual movement known as the Enlightenment. It emphasized reason, the scientific method, and individualism. As a result of this new thinking, some people questioned the role of monarchs in their lives.

Rejecting Rulers

Many people wanted a say in their government. In the British colonies of North America, people refused to accept King George III as their king by divine right. In 1776 they declared independence, forming the United States of America.

In 1789 in France, workers and the poor took action to improve their lives. They formed a National Assembly, which

Educational Video

Scan here for a video on the modern countries that still have monarchies:

passed the Declaration of the Rights of Man and of the Citizen. This document stated that all people "are born and remain free and equal in rights." No one—not even the king—could take away these rights. In the years that followed, France experienced political upheaval and violence. Many members of the aristocracy were beheaded. Eventually the monarchy was abolished and, in 1793, King Louis XVI and his wife, Queen Marie Antoinette, were executed.

Enlightened Monarchs

Some rulers welcomed leaders of the Enlightenment into their courts and were inspired to institute reforms in their government. One of them was the king of Prussia, Frederick II, who reigned from 1740 to 1786. He became famous for establishing bureaucratic reforms that made the Prussian civil service more efficient, and for codifying the law. Also known as Frederick the Great, the Prussian king referred to himself as "the first servant of the state."

Other enlightened monarchs typically allowed religious toleration, freedom of speech and the press, and the right to hold private property. They worked to build stronger nations by reforming laws. Most of these monarchs, who included Catherine II of Russia and Carlos III of Spain, developed programs to advance education, science, and the arts.

Royal Relations

In the late 1700s, Britain was an industrial and military power. At the same time, its military might, particularly its naval strength, led to the growth of an empire. By the late 1800s the British Empire controlled much of the globe, from Iraq to India, from large parts of Africa to Australia.

The period in which Queen Victoria ruled Great Britain, from 1837 to 1901, is known as the Victorian era.

Queen Victoria, who succeeded to the throne in June 1837, ruled the British Empire at its peak.

In 1840 Victoria married a prince of two dukedoms in Germany, Albert of Saxe-Coburg-Gotha. They would have nine children, many of whom married into other royal families of Europe. The queen ruled until January 1901, a span of more than 63 years.

Victoria is sometimes called the grandmother of Europe. At the turn of the 20th century her son King Edward VII was the uncle of the German emperor Kaiser Wilhelm II; Tsar Nicholas II of Russia; King Alfonso XIII of Spain; and Carl Eduard, Duke of Saxe-Coburg-Gotha. The British king was brother-in-law to George I of the Hellenes (the king of Greece) and King Frederick VIII of Denmark. And Edward was cousin to the kings of Belgium, Portugal, and Bulgaria, and to the queen of the Netherlands.

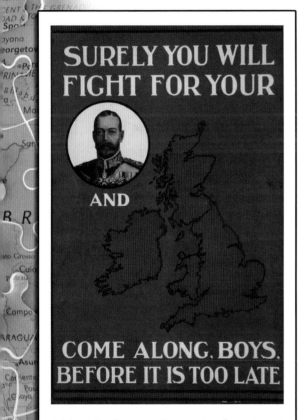

This British recruiting poster from 1915 appeals to young men to fight for their monarch, King George V, and their country during the First World War. Britain was allied with France and Russia.

World War I

After sitting on the British throne for just nine years, Edward VII died in 1910. His son George V succeeded him.

Four years later, in 1914, the heir to the Austro-Hungarian Empire was murdered at Sarajevo by a Serbian nationalist. The assassination of Archduke Franz Ferdinand led to a huge conflict that engulfed Europe.

On one side of the war were the Central Powers: Germany, the Austro-Hungarian Empire, the Ottoman Empire, and the Kingdom of Bulgaria. They were opposed by the Allies, including

Great Britain, France, Russia, and later the United States. The Great War, later known as World War I, would last until 1918 and claim the lives of more than 10 million soldiers.

The Central Powers suffered defeat, and they paid the price with the loss of their monarchies. In 1918 Germany's Kaiser Wilhelm II was forced to *abdicate*, and the monarchy was abolished. That same year saw the end of the monarchy of the Austro-Hungarian Empire when Emperor Karl I was deposed.

Other monarchies fell as a direct or indirect result of World War I. Russia's Tsar Nicholas had been forced to abdicate in 1917, and he and his family were murdered the following year. In 1922

Nicholas II, the last tsar of Russia, with his oldest son Alexei, the heir apparent, circa 1914. A 1917 revolution in Russia forced Nicholas II to give up the throne, and he was imprisoned with his family. In 1918 they were executed, ending the Romanov dynasty of Russian tsars.

Sultan Mehmed VI was forced from power and the Ottoman *sultanate* abolished. The Greek monarchy was abolished in 1924 (although it would be restored in 1935.)

World War II

The Second World War, which began in 1939, would alter monarchies in Japan and Italy. The two countries, along with

Old Monarchy

The oldest monarchy in Europe is in Denmark. It was established in the early 10th century by Gorm the Old, a warrior chief who unified clans into the kingdom of Denmark. Denmark became a constitutional monarchy in 1849.

Germany, formed the Axis, which fought the Allies (principally Great Britain, France, the Soviet Union, and the United States). When World War II ended in 1945, one monarchy would be abolished and the other greatly diminished.

In Italy a constitutional monarchy had been established, under the royal House of Savoy, in 1861. During the 1920s, however, King Victor Emmanuel III had allowed Benito Mussolini to eliminate Italy's democratic institutions and create a fascist dictatorship. In June 1946, after their country's defeat in World War II, Italian citizens held a popular *referendum* in which they voted to abolish the monarchy. Italy became a republic.

In the 19th century, during a period of political upheaval known as the Meiji Restoration, Japan had reestablished its monarchy, with the emperor as absolute ruler. As in the past, the emperor claimed divine ancestry. Emperor Meiji, who ruled from 1867 to 1912, and his sons were regarded as god-kings.

This belief in the divine emperor still held when the grandson of Meiji, Emperor Hirohito, held the throne during World War II. After Japan's defeat in 1945, the monarchy was not dissolved. But the emperor was forced to renounce the idea that Japan's imperial rulers were gods. And he had to accept his role as laid out in a new constitution—that the emperor was only a symbolic leader, with no political power.

The Commonwealth

The British monarchy continued after World War II. But the British Empire decreased dramatically in size as its many colonies, protectorates, and territories became independent. During the reign of King George VI, who ruled from 1936 to 1952, India and Pakistan gained independence. Upon his death Elizabeth II ascended to the throne. In the years that followed, new countries emerged from British lands in Asia (such as Sri Lanka), Africa (including Ghana, Kenya, and Nigeria), and the Caribbean (such as Trinidad and Tobago). Many of these independent countries joined the Commonwealth of Nations, an

During her reign Queen Elizabeth has regularly visited each of the Commonweatlth realms, although her schedule of international travel has slowed as she has grown older.

intergovernmental organization mostly made up of former colonies of the British Empire. Queen Elizabeth serves as its ceremonial head.

In addition to ruling the United Kingdom, Elizabeth II is also monarch and head of state of 15 parliamentary democracies that remain as Commonwealth realms. They include Australia, Belize, Canada, Jamaica, and New Zealand.

Royal Equality

During the second half of the 20th century, several monarchies in Europe opened the door for women. The first-born child, regardless of gender, would legally have the right to the throne.

For centuries European monarchies abided by Salic law, which prohibited females and descendants in the female line from inheriting land, titles, and offices. In 1953 the constitution in Denmark was revised to allow a woman to ascend to the throne. In 1980 Sweden became the first European monarchy to declare equal primogeniture. This means that the crown goes to the eldest child, regardless of gender. The Netherlands, Norway, and Belgium followed suit. And in October 2011 all 16 countries that are realms of the British Commonwealth approved similar reform in royal succession.

Monarchies in Asia

Like Japan, the countries of Cambodia, Bhutan, and Thailand (formerly known as Siam) have hereditary monarchies. They are also constitutional monarchies. The Kingdom of Cambodia is a restored monarchy that was reinstated in 1993 within a multi-party democracy. The Himalayan nation of Bhutan became a

constitutional monarchy in 2008, when King Jigme Khesar Namgyel Wangchuck ratified a constitution transferring much of his power to the Council of Cabinet Ministers.

The ancient monarchy of Siam, founded in 1350, became a constitutional monarchy in 1932 after a bloodless military coup. Maha Vajiralongkorn became king of Thailand in October 2016. He succeeded his father, Bhumibol Adulyadej, who had ruled Thailand for more than 70 years. Most Thais regard their king with reverence, and strict rules prohibit anyone from criticizing members of the royal family.

Malaysia is considered a federal parliamentary democracy with a constitutional monarch. Hereditary monarchs, or sultans, govern 9 of the 13 states that make up the federation of Malaysia. The sultans select a king, or "Paramount Ruler," who serves a five-year term as ceremonial head of state.

Nearby Brunei is an absolute monarchy. Its 1959 constitution established the sultan as the head of state with full executive authority. The same family has ruled the sultanate, official-

The Sultan of Brunei is the wealthiest monarch in the world, with a personal fortune estimated at about $20 billion in 2018.

King Abdullah II of Jordan attends a conference of the League of Arab States. Although Jordan has a constitutional monarchy, Abdullah still holds considerable power over the country's government.

ly named the Malay Islamic Monarchy, for more than six centuries. Hassanal Bolkiah has ruled the country since 1967.

Monarchies in the Middle East

A few Middle Eastern countries are constitutional monarchies. But their rulers are not ceremonial figureheads. The leaders of Bahrain, Jordan, and Kuwait tend to hold greater powers than constitutional monarchs do in most other parts of the world.

For example, in Jordan the king has real political power. He appoints the country's prime minister and cabinet and can dis-

solve Parliament. Members of the Hashemite family have sat on the throne since the 1921 founding of the Emirate of Transjordan, a British protectorate. In 1946 Transjordan gained independence from Britain was renamed the Hashemite Kingdom of Jordan. The royal family claims to being descended from the Arab chieftain Quraysh, who was a descendant of the Prophet Muhammad. Thus, the Hashemites claim direct descent from the founder of Islam. King Abdullah II has reigned in Jordan since 1999.

Salman bin Abdul-Aziz Al Saud became king of Saudi Arabia in 2015. He is a son of the country's founder, King Abdul-Aziz.

In the constitutional emirate of Kuwait the amir (an alternate spelling of emir) serves both as the head of state and the head of government. He has the last word on government policies. He also has the power to dissolve the National Assembly, although the constitution requires that new elections be held within 60 days. Kuwait has been under the rule of the Al Sabah family since the mid-18th century.

In countries with absolute monarchies, the rulers typically serve as both head of state and government leader. In Oman, for example, Sultan Qaboos is both sultan and prime minister.

(He also heads the foreign, defense, and finance ministries of the government.) In Saudi Arabia the king is the chief of state and head of government.

The Kingdom of Saudi Arabia is named after the ruling Al Saud family. King Abdul-Aziz established Saudi Arabia in 1932. Following his death in 1953, he has been succeeded by his sons. (In Saudia Arabia the throne usually passes to the monarch's next eldest brother.) Abdullah bin Abdul-Aziz Al Saud succeeded his half-brother King Fahd, in August 2005. Abdullah had governed as *regent* since 1998, when Fahd suffered a debilitating stroke. When King Abdullah died in 2015, he was succeeded by another half-brother, Salman bin Abdul-Aziz Al Saud. In 2017, the 81-year-old king announced that his 32-year-old son Mohammad bin Salman Al Saud would become crown prince, making Mohammad first in line for the Saudi throne. If and when Mohammad bin Salman takes the crown, he would be the first grandson of King Abdul-Aziz to rule the kingdom.

Another absolute monarchy is Qatar, an emirate that has been ruled by the Al Thani family since the mid-1800s. In 1995 Crown Prince Hamad bin Khalifa deposed his father to become emir. He subsequently introduced many reforms, including a

 Saudi Ceremony

During the traditional Islamic investiture ceremony, Saudi kings receive an oath of allegiance, or *bay'ah*, from tribal chiefs, Islamic clerics, and other prominent Saudis. In 2015, when Salman officially became king, hundreds participated in the ceremony. Each person shook hands with Salman while saying, "I express my allegiance to you. I hear and obey, except in what would disobey Allah."

constitution providing for a Shura (consultative) council. In 2013, Sheikh Hamad abdicated the Qatari throne in favor of his son, Tamim bin Hamad. Since coming to power, Sheikh Tamim has directed the government to upgrade roads and infrastructure within Qatar, and embark on projects that help ordinary people. The sheikh has also attempted to diversify the economy, which is dominated by the production of oil and natural gas.

Sheikh Tamim and other monarchs in the Arab world have focused on keeping their people happy in part because of civil unrest that shook the Arab world. Beginning in 2011, hundreds of thousands of people living in Arab countries took part in rallies and protests in an effort to bring about political reform. This movement has been referred to as the "Arab Spring."

In countries with monarchies, demonstrators called on leaders to make constitutional reforms. Among their demands were calls for limits on the monarch's authority and increases in the powers of elected legislatures. The protests led some kings to promise certain political reforms. However, little meaningful reform has taken place so far.

Usefulness of the Monarchy

At the turn of the 20th century, monarchy was the most common form of government. Today most governments are republics. There are fewer than 45 monarchal governments. And most of them are constitutional ones.

Critics of monarchy call it a relic that is no longer relevant in modern times. They complain that figurehead rulers of constitutional monarchies cannot accomplish much because they have no real political power.

Emperor Akihito and Empress Michiko of Japan stand at the entrance to an imperial residence. The emperor is a symbol of Japan and opens the parliament session each year, but has no real role or influence over the government.

Supporters counter that members of royal families often play important ambassadorial and ceremonial roles in government. And they often do good, by supporting or serving as spokespersons for charitable groups.

In Britain, the monarchy has many fans. The interest and celebration over the 2011 wedding of Prince William and Kate Middleton, or the sapphire jubilee of Queen Elizabeth II in 2017, showed that the British monarchy continues to make a powerful and direct connection with the people of the United Kingdom. Polls indicate that approximately 70 to 75 percent of

Britons support keeping the monarchy.

Many citizens have great faith in the institution, and consider it part of their identity. When asked whether the monarchy was necessary, one woman told the *Christian Science Monitor*, "The queen will hold things together. I can't imagine England without a monarchy, it wouldn't be England anymore!"

 Text-Dependent Questions

1. Under Japan's 1947 constitution, what role does the emperor have?
2. What family has ruled Kuwait since the mid-18th century?

 Research Project

Using your school library or the internet, find out how the king or emir of an Arab state such as Jordan, Morocco, Kuwait, or Saudi Arabia has responded to the Arab Spring protests. What, if anything, did these rules promise to do? What, if any, meaningful reforms of the political system have been implemented? Write a two-page paper.

Series Glossary of Key Terms

autonomy—the right of self-government.

aristocracy—an elite or upper class of society whose members hold hereditary titles or offices; a ruling class or nobility.

BCE and CE—an alternative to the traditional Western designation of calendar eras, which used the birth of Jesus as a dividing line. BCE stands for "Before the Common Era," and is equivalent to BC ("Before Christ"). Dates labeled CE, or "Common Era," are equivalent to *Anno Domini* (AD, or "the Year of Our Lord").

civil society—the sum total of institutions, organizations, and groups promoting social and civic causes in a country (for example, human rights groups, labor unions, arts foundations) that are not funded or controlled by the government or business interests.

colonialism—control or domination by one country over an area or people outside its boundaries; the policy of colonizing foreign lands.

communism—a system in which property and goods are owned or controlled by the state.

democracy—a system of government in which political authority is retained by the people, who exercise this authority through voting.

ideology—a system of beliefs, values, and ideas forming the basis of a social, economic, or political philosophy.

monarchy—a system of government in which a monarch reigns over a state or territory, usually for life and by hereditary right.

nationalism—the belief that shared ethnicity, language, and history should form the basis for political organization; the desire of people with a common culture to have their own state.

oligarchy—a form of government in which a small group of people holds power, often for their own benefit.

plutocracy—a form of government in which the very wealthy rule.

self-determination—determination by a people of their own future political status.

theocracy—a system of government in which religious leaders rule in the name of God or a deity.

totalitarianism—an extreme form of authoritarianism in which the state seeks to control all aspects of citizens' lives.

Chronology

4000 BCE: Monarchy emerges as a form of government in large urban civilizations.

CE 800: Charlemagne is crowned king of what will later become the Holy Roman Empire.

1215: Rebellious barons force King John of England to sign the Magna Carta, a document establishing that the king is not above the rule of law.

1517: Beginning of Protestant Reformation in Europe, which creates religious and political unrest.

1689: British Parliament passes the Bill of Rights, which establishes a constitutional monarchy in England.

1789: Beginning of the French Revolution, which will eventually lead to the abolishment of France's monarchy.

1914–18: World War I leads to the abolishment of monarchies in Germany, Russia, Austria-Hungary, and other countries.

1945: With the end of World War II the Japanese emperor is forced to accept a symbolic role in a constitutional monarchy.

1952: Queen Elizabeth II ascends the British throne following the death of her father, George VI.

1970: Qaboos bin Said al Said becomes sultan of Oman.

1999: In February, Abdullah II succeeds his father, Hussein, as king of Jordan.

2013: Willem-Alexander becomes king of the Netherlands, following the abdication of his mother, Queen Beatrix.

2015: In January, Salman bin Abdulaziz Al Saud becomes ruler of Saudi Arabia. In September, Queen Elizabeth II becomes the longest-serving monarch in British history, surpassing her great-great-grandmother Queen Victoria.

2016: King Bhumibol Adulyadej of Thailand dies at the age of 88. At the time of his death, he was the world's longest-reigning monarch, having ruled Thailand for 70 years.

2017: Queen Elizabeth II becomes the first British monarch to celebrate a Sapphire Jubilee, marking 65 years on the throne.

2018: Forty-five countries have monarchs as the head of state.

Further Reading

Carter, Miranda. *George, Nicholas and Wilhelm: Three Royal Cousins and the Road to World War One*. New York: Alfred A. Knopf, 2010.

Freeman, Philip. *Alexander the Great*. New York: Simon & Schuster, 2011.

Jobson, Robert. *The Future Royal Family: William, Kate and the Modern Royals*. London: Overamstel, 2017.

Lee, Christopher. *Monarchy: Past, Present . . . and Future?* London: Bene Factum, 2014.

Robinson, Francis. *The Mughal Emperors: And the Islamic Dynasties of India, Iran, Central Asia, 1206–1925*. London: Thames & Hudson, 2007.

Siler, Julia Flynn. *Lost Kingdom: Hawaii's Last Queen, the Sugar Kings, and America's First Imperial Adventure*. New York: Atlantic Monthly Press, 2012.

Internet Resources

www.royal.gov.uk

The official website of the British Monarchy provides the latest news about the royal family, as well as links to the history of the monarchy, the royal collection and residences, and much more.

www.royaltymonarchy.com/sovereigns/0000world.html

This website provides a list of the countries that still have monarchies, as well as the name of the current ruling king or queen.

www.kinghussein.gov.jo/hash_intro.html

The website for the Hashemite royal family of Jordan features links to the family tree and provides background information on Islam and the royal coat of arms.

Publisher's Note: The websites listed on this page were active at the time of publication. The publisher is not responsible for websites that have changed their address or discontinued operation since the date of publication. The publisher reviews and updates the websites each time the book is reprinted.

Chapter Notes

p. 22:   "What is the king . . ." Angela Thomas, *Egyptian Gods and Myths* (London: Shire Publications, 2001), p. 25.

p. 45:   "The just and peaceful . . ." Neil MacGregor, *A History of the World in 100 Objects* (New York: Viking, 2011), p. 344.

p. 64:   "I know I have . . ." Modern History Sourcebook, "Queen Elizabeth I: Against the Spanish Armada, 1588." http://www.fordham.edu/halsall/mod/1588elizabeth.asp

p. 64:   "[Kings are] God's anointed . . ." John Edmund Cox, ed., *Miscellaneous Writings and Letters of Thomas Cranmer* (Vancouver, B.C., Canada: Regent College Publishing, 2001), p. 126.

p. 65:   "Kings are justly called gods . . ." Suzanne McIntire and William E. Burns, *Speeches in World History* (New York: Facts on File, 2009), p. 137.

p. 70:   "are born and remain . . ." The Avalon Project, "Declaration of the Rights of Man—1789." http://avalon.law.yale.edu/18th_century/rightsof.asp

p. 80:   "I express my . . ." "Clerics, Chiefs Pledge Loyalty to New Saudi King," msnbc.com, August 3, 2005. http://www.msnbc.msn.com/id/8793922/ns/world_news-mideast_n_africa/t/clerics-chiefs-pledge-loyalty-new-saudi-king/#.T0Zzx5jN6kI

p. 83:   "The queen will hold . . ." Robert Marquand, "As William and Kate Await Honeymoon, Britain's Monarchy Enjoys Its Own," *Christian Science Monitor* (May 6, 2011).

SZENT KORONA ÉS KORONÁZÁSI JELVÉNYEK
MÁSOLATAI

1966

Rézötvözet, ékkő, gyöngy, zománc, üveg
Készítő: Bartha Lajos
Korona: 22,8 x 19 x 21,8 cm
Jogar: 38 x 7,5 cm
Országalma: 17,5 x 9,5 cm

REPRODUCTIONS OF THE HOLY CROWN
AND CORONATION REGALIA

1966

Copper alloy, gems, pearls, enamel, glass
Made by Lajos Bartha
Crown: 22,8 x 19 x 21,8 cm
Sceptre: 38 x 7,5 cm
Orb: 17,5 x 9,5 cm

Index

Numbers in **bold italic** refer to captions.

Contributors

Larry Gillespie is a graduate of the University of Maryland. He lives and works in the Washington, D.C., area. He is the author of several books for young adults.

Picture Credits: Everett Collection: 71; Library of Congress: 72, 73; © Photos.com, a division of Getty Images: 28, 50, 52, 54, 62, 63, 67; used under license from Shutterstock, Inc.: 1, 2, 7, 9, 15, 16, 18, 21, 23, 26, 27, 31, 32, 34, 36, 39, 44, 57, 58, 75; Atlaspix / Shutterstock.com: 91; Art Babych / Shutterstock.com: 12; Fotokon / Shutterstock.com: 82; Michelangeloop / Shutterstock.com: 40; Paolo Paradiso / Shutterstock.com: 92; Gokhan Yasin UYSAL / Shutterstock.com: 47; United Nations photo: 11, 77, 78, 79; Wikimedia Commons: 42, 60.

BW

OCT / - 2022

W9-ACK-912